PRIČA O BROJEVIMA

THE NUMBER STORY

SMALL BOOK ONE

ENGLISH - BOSNIAN

*Numbers Teach Children
Their Number Names*

written and illustrated by

MISS ANNA

Early Reader Edition of *The Number Story 1*
Bronze Medal Winner, 2016 Wishing Shelf Book Award

Cover by | Lumpy Publishing
Layout by | Lumpy Publishing
Translated by Aljoša P.
Coloring by Jieeun Woo and Maria Mirabella

Library of Congress Control Number: 2018902040

Names: Miss Anna, author.
Title: Number story : numbers teach children their number names / Miss Anna.
Description: Portland, OR: Lumpy Publishing, 2018.
Identifiers: ISBN 978-1-945977-83-1| LCCN 2018902040
Summary: The pictures and rhymes present stories which introduce numbers 0-10.
Subjects: LCSH Numeration—English--Bosnian--Pictorial works--Juvenile literature. | BISAC JUVENILE NONFICTION /
JUVENILE NONFICTION /
Languages: English--Bosnian
Classification: LCC QA141.3 .M57 2018 | DDC 513—dc23

Publisher: Lumpy Publishing
Website: www.missannabooks.com
Email: missanna@missannabooks.com

Paperback: ISBN 978-1-945977-83-1
Printed in the U.S.A.   1 3 5 7 9 10 8 6 4 2

Želite li da naučite naše brojeve?

It is very easy and a lot of fun!

Lako i je zaista zanimljivo!

Say-along our little jingle

Hajde, pjevajte sa nama!

starting from Number One!

Krenimo sa brojem Jedan!

1

ONE looks like my one finger.

JEDAN

je prav kao moj prst.

ONE!
JEDAN!

2

TWO trails a tail.

DVA

ima dugačak rep.

A TAIL! REP!

3

THREE has bumps.

TRI

je krivudav poput brda.

Pogledajte njegova zelena brda!

4

FOUR carries a sail.

ČETIRI

ima jedro kao brod.

4
A SAIL!
JEDRO KAO BROD!

5

FIVE   is a racing track.

PET

je kao staza za trkanje.

VRooom
BRMM!

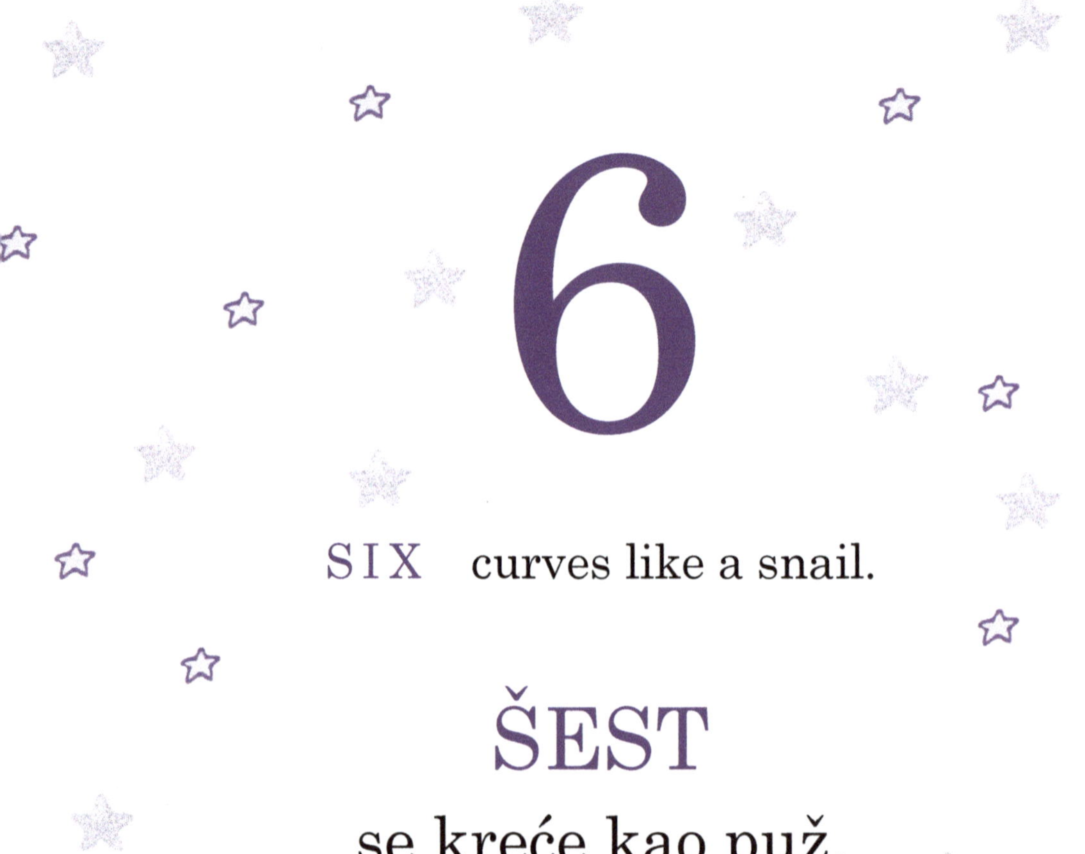

6

SIX curves like a snail.

ŠEST

se kreće kao puž.

A SNAIL! PUŽ!

7
SEVEN has a sharp angle.
SEDAM
ima oštar ugao.

OUCH!
PAZI!
OŠTRO!

8

E I G H T   is rollercoaster rails.

OSAM

je kao tobogan.

JUHU!
YIPPEE!

9

NINE is a bubble on a stick.

DEVET

izgleda kao balon na štapu.

A BUBBLE! BALON!

10

TEN   is an eye of a whale.

DESET

izgleda kao kitovo oko.

MIG MIG!
WINK!
HELLO!   ZDRAVO!

And I **O**

ZERO is an empty pail.

NULA

je kao prazna kanta.

IT'S EMPTY!
NIŠTA! PRAZNA!

Thank you for playing with us today.

We had a lot of fun too!

Hvala što ste se igrali sa nama.

I nama je bilo zanimljivo!

We are your Number friends,
Zero to Ten,
Who will be here for you~
Mi smo brojevi
i tvoji smo drugari.
Mi smo uvijek uz tebe~

Bye-bye now!
See you again soon!
Doviđenja za sada!
Vidimo se opet!

The Numbers are *SINGING* too!

To sing-a-long, look for Miss Anna Number Story
at your favorite music store like iTUNES.

MP3

| Numbers 0-10
IDENTIFYING
& COUNTING | Numbers 11-20
& Ordinals
first, second, third... | Numbers 0-100
& Place Values
ones, tens, hundreds... | About Clocks
& Telling Time
hours, minutes, seconds... |

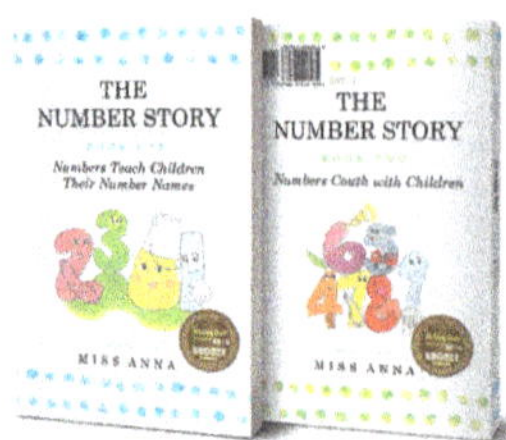

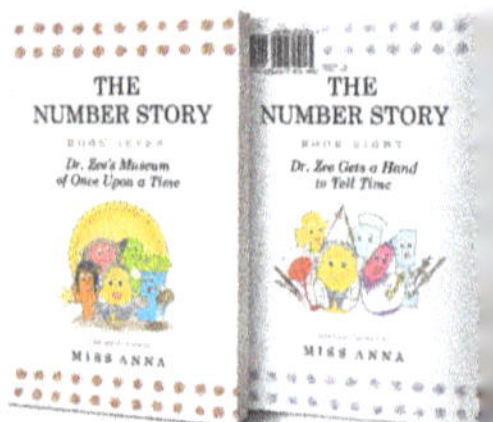

Number Story 1 & 2

isbn: 978-0-996216-48-7

Number Story 3 & 4

isbn: 978-1-945977-01-5

Number Story 5 & 6

isbn: 978-1-945977-06-0

Number Story 7 & 8

isbn: 978-1-949320-40-4

For more Miss Anna books to love,
visit us at

www.missannabooks.com

Numbers are working hard all over the world!
Come Travel the World with Us!